The Easter Stranger

The Easter Story, Luke 24:1–35, for Children

Written by Nicole E. Dreyer

Illustrated by Len Ebert

CONCORDIA PUBLISHING HOUSE • SAINT LOUIS

Two friends were on a dusty road
They walked along, their heads hung low.
Their sadness would not go away;
They could not figure out this day.

Just two sad friends—then there were three!
From where did He come? Who is He?
A Stranger whom they did not know
Had joined them on that dusty road.

"You look so sad," the Stranger said.
"Why do you walk with drooping heads?
Tell Me what happened here today.
Please tell your tale along the way."

The two could not believe their ears.
Who is this Man who just appeared?
How is it that He doesn't know
The things that caused them so much woe?

Cleopas shook his head and said,
"Our best Friend, Jesus, now is dead!
They nailed Him high upon a tree
Placed on a hill called Calvary.

"And since they laid Him in the grave,
Time has passed; it's been three long days!
He's not the One sent to redeem;
With Jesus died our hopes and dreams."

And then they said, "We're so confused,
Because the women say they viewed
Angels who said He is alive!
But we've not seen Him with our eyes."

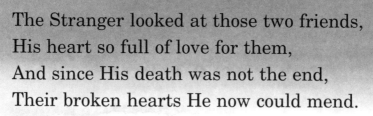

The Stranger looked at those two friends,
His heart so full of love for them,
And since His death was not the end,
Their broken hearts He now could mend.

So as they walked, the Man began
To tell them of God's mighty plan.
He said that Jesus came to die
So we could live with Him on high.

Our Lord's sweet death forgives our sins;
The fight with death our Lord did win!
For as the prophets' words have said:
"The Christ will be raised from the dead!"

The friends now smiled and raised their heads,
No longer sad or filled with dread.
And joy now filled their hearts again;
The Stranger had become their Friend.

"The hour is late, dear Friend," they said.
"Come stay with us; come break our bread.
And tell us more as we walk down
This dusty road to the next town."

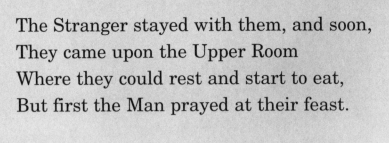

The Stranger stayed with them, and soon,
They came upon the Upper Room
Where they could rest and start to eat,
But first the Man prayed at their feast.

And then their eyes were opened wide;
The Stranger's face began to shine!
The Father's glory from Him shone,
And Jesus' presence now was known.

And when He'd vanished from that place,
They said, "Our hearts began to race
When He joined us on our walk today
And talked with us along the way."

"Come unto Me," our Savior says,
"And rest on Me your weary head.
I now have all your debt repaid;
Believe in Me, and you are saved."

Dear Parents,

"We had hoped that He was the one" (Luke 24:21).

Jesus had turned the world upside down with His teaching and His miracles. When it got to be too much for His enemies, they conspired to put an end to Him. His enemies as well as His followers watched Him die. Then, it was discovered that His body was gone. The tomb was empty. Their grief at Jesus' death was compounded by confusion.

This was big news. How could it be that the Stranger on the road to Emmaus didn't know these things? Oh, but this Stranger did know things. He reminded the disciples that the Christ had to suffer these things to fulfill the Old Testament prophecies. Didn't He tell them so Himself?

The Stranger accepted the invitation to join the disciples for the evening. And then, during their meal, they recognized Him as Jesus—and He disappeared. These events took place the same day that Jesus rose from the grave.

This Bible story helps to reinforce that Jesus promises to be with us always. When bad things happen, when we are so sad that we don't really see what's going on around us—Jesus is with us. Just like the Stranger reminded the disciples that God had promised to send a Savior, this Bible story reminds us that Jesus is that Savior.

The Editor

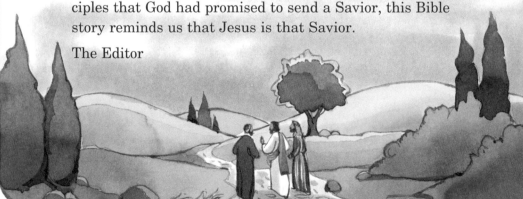